Bible Readers Series

A Study of Proverbs

FINDING THE WAY OF LIFE

Frank Johnson

Abingdon Press / Nashville

**FINDING THE WAY OF LIFE
A STUDY OF PROVERBS**

*Copyright © 1990 by Cokesbury.
Abingdon Press edition published 2002.*

Scripture quotations in this publication, unless otherwise indicated, are from the New Revised Standard Version of the Bible, copyrighted © 1989 by the Division of Christian Education of the National Council of the Churches of Christ in the United States of America, and are used by permission.

Lessons are based on the International Sunday School Lessons for Christian Teaching, copyright © 1986, by the Committee on the Uniform Series. Text excerpted from *Adult Bible Studies,* Summer 1990.

This book is printed on acid-free paper.

ISBN 0-687-05133-9

02 03 04 05 06 07 08 09 10 11—10 9 8 7 6 5 4 3 2 1
Manufactured in the United States of America.

CONTENTS

Chapter One

THE BEGINNING OF KNOWLEDGE

PURPOSE

To help us discover that faith in God leads to true wisdom and to moral living

BIBLE PASSAGE

Proverbs 1:1-9, 20-23

1 The proverbs of Solomon son of David, king of Israel:

2 For learning about wisdom and
        instruction,
    for understanding words of insight,
3 for gaining instruction in wise dealing,
    righteousness, justice, and equity;
4 to teach shrewdness to the simple,
    knowledge and prudence to the young—
5 let the wise also hear and gain in
        learning,
    and the discerning acquire skill,
6 to understand a proverb and a figure,
    the words of the wise and their riddles.

7 The fear of the LORD is the

beginning of knowledge;
    fools despise wisdom and instruction.

8 Hear, my child, your father's
        instruction,
    and do not reject your mother's teaching;
9 for they are a fair garland for your
        head,
    and pendants for your neck. . . .

20 Wisdom cries out in the street;
    in the squares she raises her voice.
21 At the busiest corner she cries out;
    at the entrance of the city gates
        she speaks:
22 "How long, O simple ones, will you love
        being simple?
  How long will scoffers delight in their scoffing
        and fools hate knowledge?
23 Give heed to my reproof;
    I will pour out my thoughts to you;
        I will make my words known to you."

CORE VERSE

The fear of the Lord *is the*
beginning of knowledge;
fools despite wisdom and instruction.

(Proverbs 1:7)

OUR NEED

On one of our many fishing trips, my father and I pulled along the shore to resupply our boat with bait and to transfer some of our fish to other containers. As we docked, my father asked me to tie up the boat. In my usual haste to get the job done, I quickly tied a knot and fastened the rope to the nearest tree. Unfortunately, the knot did not hold for long. Our boat quickly began to move out into the lake. By the time we noticed, the boat was well away from the dock.

"I thought I told you to tie up the boat," my father said.

"I did," said I.

"I guess your knot wasn't very strong or else you didn't tie it to something very secure," he said.

"I guess not," I replied.

Human behavior often floats aimlessly on a lake of changing circumstances unless it is attached to strong ethical conviction. The Book of Proverbs provides a manual of moral instruction for proper conduct. It is a guide to living a happy, successful life in compliance with God's moral law. The values the Book of Proverbs describes and encourages were derived from years of human experience and are sanctioned by God. That is, proper moral conduct is an expression of religious faith.

In Proverbs, faith in God and in his divinely established moral order stimulates knowledge and understanding. For the wise persons who collected and arranged these sayings, the fear of God always preceded and stimulated knowledge and morality. Because of their faith in God, people knew what was true and did what was right. They were not afloat on a lake, moved about by the wind. They knew what was expected of them, and they had a basis for determining right from wrong.

FAITHFUL LIVING

Proverbs 1:1 identifies the following material as "The proverbs of Solomon son of David, king of Israel." Although Proverbs appears to be a collection of literary sayings and poems from many sources rather than from one writer, the dedication to Solomon as the source is appropriate, since

Solomon was a patron of the wisdom tradition of early Israel.

Verses 2-6 indicate the purposes of the sayings that follow. They are to provide instruction in general knowledge, in morality, and in faith. To be more specific, these sayings join together those three areas, climaxing in the affirmation that true knowledge begins with faith (verse 7). The expression "fear of the LORD" refers to a reverence for God's natural and moral laws that are woven into the fabric of nature and of human relationships. As surely as one experiences the fact of gravity, so also does one confront the reality of the consequences that follow certain actions:

> Those who till their land will have
> plenty of food,
> but those who follow worthless
> pursuits have no sense.
> (Proverbs 12:11)

It is entirely appropriate that the person or persons who collected and arranged Proverbs into its final form recognized faith as the foundation for genuine knowledge and proper morality. Faith provides the proper framework within which knowledge is to be achieved and used; faith identifies certain values as worthy of human effort. Moral virtues such as "wise dealing," "righteousness," "justice," "equity," "prudence," and so on are proper expressions of piety (Proverbs 1:3-4). Likewise, acquiring the skills to understand proverbs, figures, and riddles suggests that true knowledge begins with an understanding of God's natural order.

Certainly, the editor of Proverbs must have known, just as we know today, that knowledge not rooted in faith can allow immoral conduct. He certainly would not have agreed with Plato's belief that knowledge equals virtue. Knowledge needs to be focused properly and used wisely. Faith provides the proper direction for knowledge. With our vast supply of knowledge today, we should remember to join knowledge to faith.

In what ways does your faith help you use your knowledge wisely?

The Companions We Choose

When I was a child, my parents constantly urged me to choose my friends carefully. "Birds of a feather flock together," they quoted frequently. Not until I had children of my own did their message really make its point with me. Regardless of whether it is fair or unfair, many people judge us by the company we keep. Even more important is the influence our companions have on our behavior.

Parents learn quickly the effects, positive and negative, of peer pressure. Early teenagers are especially vulnerable to what their friends say, think, and do. Many times teenagers who have experimented with alcohol or other drugs have done so because their friends were doing the same thing. On the other side, however, friends can provide support and encouragement. They can be as positive an influence as they can be negative. Either way, our companions exert tremendous influences on us and on our children.

To teach the dangers of associating with evil companions, the editor of Proverbs starts with a lengthy admonition. The central theme of this unit (1:8-19) is the command in verse 10 not to join a group of evil companions. The opening reference (1:8) to parents as the source of these teachings reflects the custom in ancient Israel of assigning to the home the task of moral instruction. Parents were not just responsible for instructing their children in virtuous conduct, the behavior of their children directly reflected on them. So it was important that parents instructed their children properly in the correct virtues.

Following the central admonition to avoid evil companions is a description of the almost irresistible enticement of the wicked (Proverbs 1:11-14). With pride, they embrace violence and death as their intimate friends. They obtain riches beyond all imagination, and they share their ill-gotten wealth. These inducements (violence, wealth, and equality) are all imaginary and disguise the wickedness of their actions. A wise person will recognize the lies of the wicked for exactly what they are.

After repeating the initial warning, the writer then offers the principal reason why the ways of violence and falsehood are not only morally wrong but also dangerous. He indicates that wickedness and violence return to take away the life of persons who perform such acts. So the evil that these persons inflict on others returns eventually to harm them. God structured the moral order of human relationships in such a way that a person's evil deeds eventually return to her or him. As you sow, so shall you reap.

The moral lesson is clear: Avoid associating with wicked companions who use violence to gain wealth. Their evil ways will return to them and take their life. The knowledge of this lesson stems from an abiding faith in God's moral laws of retribution. Divine justice will prevail always. Faith provides a clear and sharp focus for knowledge and for moral conduct.

What examples of evil returning to evildoers that have affected you or your community can you share?

Heeding Wisdom's Call

Moral instruction in ancient Israel came from many lips. In Proverbs 1:8-19, parents teach their child the value of avoiding evil companions. In verses 20-33, a sage offers all persons instructions on the virtues of good behavior. Here wisdom is personified as a woman.

Personification refers to the literary technique of attributing personal qualities and behaviors to ideas. For instance, we often hear the expression, "Justice is blind." By attributing the human characteristic of blindness to the concept of justice, we understand more readily the intention of the writer or speaker.

The writers of the Old Testament, as well as other writers in the ancient Near East, were familiar with this literary technique. Personification is used to intensify the colors of nature and to transform inanimate objects into persons. Beginning in verse 20, wisdom is personified as a female prophet who delivers God's words of salvation (knowledge) to anyone who will listen.

The writer's choice to personify wisdom as a female prophet illustrates the important role of women in ancient Israel. Women, no less than their male counterparts, functioned as messengers for God. Like their husbands, wives shared the responsibility for educating children. Women were given proper respect. Gender stereotypes had no place among God's messengers then nor do they now.

How are women given respect in your community?

Wisdom

In the passages from Proverbs 1, wisdom stations herself at the busy crossroads of the city. Wherever people can be found, wisdom is present to proclaim her message of salvation from God. She brings true wisdom that leads to knowledge and to virtuous living. The consequence of heeding her call is abundant life, blessed by God.

Unfortunately, many people ignore wisdom's cries. These people refuse to listen to her counsel; and, as a result, they are doomed for disaster. Wisdom brings not only God's words of salvation but also God's words of judgment. The kind of salvation she brings is true knowledge of God's moral order. Such wisdom results in the proper behavior that leads to the good life. In contrast, the fool who arrogantly refuses to listen to wisdom faces certain calamity.

Today, when electronic information systems provide us with unlimited information, it is more important than ever to distinguish between true wisdom that comes from God and the false knowledge furnished by human imagination. We are gathering more and more knowledge about ourselves, about the social structures that surround us, and about the physical world in which we live. Medical procedures that are commonplace were science fiction two decades ago. Micro-computers receive and process information with astonishing speed. We are living in the midst of an explosion of knowledge.

How are we using this knowledge? Do we have new value systems to evaluate this information? What social structures have we created to ensure that we use this knowledge properly? Have we formulated ways to determine ethical answers to complicated medical and legal issues? What basic ethical values serve as our standards for determining right and wrong? In what respects are we better off today than we were twenty-five years ago? In what ways are things worse now than they were before?

To return to the central theme of Proverbs 1, religious faith provides the only true source of wisdom; and, hence, it offers the only proper way to consider and to adopt ethical values. Religious faith enables us to use knowledge wisely in the ways that are pleasing to God. The moral values that we acquire from our Christian faith give proper shape and direction to our knowledge.

CLOSING PRAYER

Eternal God, make us sensitive to your wisdom and values. Grant us the insight to understand, the trust to believe, and the courage to act. Through Jesus Christ our Lord, we pray. Amen.

Chapter Two

THE PRIORITY OF WISDOM

PURPOSE

To challenge us to embrace the ways of wisdom that lead to abundant living

BIBLE PASSAGE

Proverbs 4:1-13

1 **Listen, children, to a father's**
   instruction,
   and be attentive, that you may gain
    insight;
2 **for I give you good precepts:**
   do not forsake my teaching.
3 **When I was a son with my father,**
   tender, and my mother's favorite,
4 **he taught me, and said to me,**
 "Let your heart hold fast my words;
   keep my commandments, and live.
5 **Get wisdom; get insight: do not forget,**
   nor turn away
   from the words of my mouth.
6 **Do not forsake her, and she will keep**
   you;
   love her, and she will guard you.

7 The beginning of wisdom is this:
   Get wisdom,
      and whatever else you get, get insight.
8 Prize her highly, and she will exalt you;
      she will honor you if you embrace her.
9 She will place on your head a fair
      garland;
      she will bestow on you a beautiful crown."

10 Hear, my child, and accept my words,
      that the years of your life may be many.
11 I have taught you the way of wisdom;
      I have led you in the paths of uprightness.
12 When you walk, your step will not be
      hampered;
      and if you run, you will not stumble.
13 Keep hold of instruction; do not let go;
      guard her, for she is your life.

CORE VERSE

The beginning of wisdom is this:
Get wisdom,
   and whatever else you get, get insight.
                              (Proverbs 4:7)

OUR NEED

One of the most important responsibilities of parents is to instill in their children a proper set of values. Studies in educational psychology indicate that most children have formed their basic codes of value by age ten. For the most part, their parents are the primary sources of these early values. As children grow into the teenage years, parental influence gives way to peer pressure. As they grow older still, social and business factors exert greater influence on their values.

Often, at some point, the church contributes in a positive way to the forming of values. Formal education in grade school, high school, and college present value systems that may impress the students. But, despite all these sources of value, the single most important influence on a child's ethical development is his or her family.

Moral education is also one of the most difficult responsibilities parents have. Recognizing that parents are a primary source for children's values is one matter; knowing which values to teach them and how to go about the task are entirely different matters.

First, parents may be confused about their own basic values. Consequently, they may send mixed signals to their children. For instance, parents tell them that cheating is wrong and telling the truth is right. Yet some parents frequently violate traffic regulations or fail to report everything on their income tax forms. Parents tell their children that drinking alcohol is wrong, yet their refrigerator contains an ample supply of beer.

A second problem is that parents may not have clear, secure, absolute standards. While many of us would acknowledge quickly that we subscribe to Christian values, we may have difficulty determining exactly which values are Christian. With so many different interpretations of Christian ethics, people often are confused. Diversity within the church over such important issues as abortion, capital punishment, genetic engineering, social justice, and so forth are perplexing to both clergy and layperson.

Those of us who struggle daily with the awesome responsibility of teaching our children morality need to look deeply at the lessons taught by Proverbs 4. Both in style and in substance, these suggestions address some of the problems mentioned above. Morality comes from wisdom. Wisdom begins with faith in God.

FAITHFUL LIVING

Proverbs 4 opens with a call to attention, typical of many instruction forms found in Proverbs. The first unit (4:1-9) actually forms an introduction to the entire chapter. It urges the student children to pursue a life of wisdom. Unlike other instructions, however, the core of this unit is an extended quotation the speaker cites from his father. Just as his father has encouraged him to follow the path of wisdom, now he instructs his children in the same tradition. By passing along the accumulated wisdom and experience of the community, parents achieved two important goals:

- youth received proper instruction in the prevailing morality and ethics of the community;
- the existing value structure of the community was secured and perpetuated.

The ethical values present in early Israelite society remained constant throughout her history. Despite differences in literary forms, the essential values transmitted in the wisdom tradition changed very little throughout Israelite history. The lessons of the past were revered and considered worthy of retention.

Although today's society is considerably larger and more complex in terms of institutional structures than was the early Israelite society, we still have certain well-established ways of transmitting and perpetuating our value systems.

We learn thinking and behaving skills through our network of public and private education. Our legal system advocates personal responsibility, respect for the rights of others, and personal self-control. The church instills reverence for God and his creation and helps us discover who we are as his children. Through our economic system we learn values of diligence, individual and cooperative effort, and pride of accomplishment. Values such as patriotism and justice are transmitted through the political institutions on local, state, and national levels.

While each of these institutional structures plays an important role in shaping our values, the family still ranks as the number one source from which young children learn essential values. This reason alone makes continuing to reinforce the family unit a crucially important matter to our society.

In Proverbs 4, the father and grandfather transmit a simple but profound message to the son: "Get wisdom" (verse 5). Judging by the warm and affectionate language they use, these teachers hold wisdom in high esteem. Expressions such as "do not forsake her," "love her," and "prize her" all convey feelings of endearment.

Wisdom is far more than an ideal, a skill, or a code of morality to these teachers. Wisdom is their beloved companion. As in any personal relationship, the beloved responds appropriately. Here, wisdom returns their affection: "she will keep you," "guard you," "exalt you," "place on your head a fair garland," and "bestow on you a beautiful crown."

Had this instruction limited its idea of wisdom to an abstract notion of morality, the attractiveness of its teaching would be diminished.

Do you think the personification technique is useful? Why or why not?

Avoiding the Path of the Wicked

The repetition of the call to attention in verse 10 indicates the beginning of a new instruction unit. The technique of compiling two or three instruction units in the same chapter is fairly commonplace in Proverbs, especially in Chapters 1–9. Frequently, the admonitions are similar in theme as well as in style.

The central theme of verses 10-19 is to follow steadfastly the ways of wisdom and to avoid, at all costs, the paths of the wicked. The father explains to his child that wisdom provides clear and forceful directions for life. The clarity of vision that wisdom provides ensures that the child will take right actions and achieve success. Likewise, wisdom will sustain and support the child when venturing into adulthood. Wisdom's gifts will adorn the child's life with beauty and strength and illuminate the child's steps so that he or she may attain all God's blessings.

By contrast, wickedness will lead the child into darkness. In his brief discourse on the nature of evil, the writer discloses several profound insights into the nature of wickedness. In verse 16, he indicates that evildoers cannot sleep if they have not done wrong. Evil becomes the staple food of their diet (verse 17).

Contemporary criminologists and prison counselors tell us that evil and violence are like malignant tumors. Once they have infected a person's system, they tend to grow and to multiply. Evil produces more evil. The more violence a person commits, the more violence he or she is likely to commit. He or she becomes willing to take greater and greater risks.

The teacher concludes his lesson by employing images of light and darkness as the consequences of righteousness and wickedness. The illumination furnished by wisdom refers to insight into God's moral law.

Certain behaviors always carry certain consequences. Thus, if a person wishes to avoid undesirable results, he or she should avoid certain acts. Likewise, the shroud of darkness that hangs about evildoers prevents them from gaining any knowledge of God's moral law. Their ignorance of the divine presence allows them to inflame the fires of their own self-destruction.

What has been your experience in dealing with wickedness and evil in human behavior? How can persons who practice such behavior be helped to change for the better?

Follow the Straight Path

The third independent unit in Chapter 4 begins with verse 20 and concludes with verse 27. Similar to the other two sub-sections in this chapter, verses 20-27 are instructional. They begin with two imperative calls to attention addressed to the child. The child is urged to pay close attention to the words that follow, to keep them ever in view, and to take them to heart.

Following the calls to attention, the speaker issues appropriate motivations for his counsel: "They are life" and "healing to all their flesh" (verse 22). Then the teacher issues specific instructions in verses 23-27. This instruction has no formal conclusion.

The same basic structure appears in numerous places in Proverbs as well as elsewhere in ancient Near Eastern wisdom literature. Since the people had a strong ethical tradition, they also had specific forms for preserving and transmitting their values. For this reason, careful readers of the Bible need to pay close attention to the literary forms as well as to the themes and ethics the texts present.

As the writer moves to the specific instructions in verses 23-27, he mentions four parts of the human body (heart, mouth [speech], eyes, feet) and assigns each one an important role to play in righteous conduct.

The heart is the central and most essential organ in the body. The ancient Israelites thought that all intellectual activity occurred in the heart. Logical activities were a function of the heart, not of the brain. The heart controlled emotions and will and shaped character. The ancient Israelites also thought that the heart was the seat of desires. Righteousness began with a heart committed to the ways of wisdom. If a person's heart was right, he or she would think and act in proper ways. So the father begins by urging his child to "keep your heart with all vigilance" (verse 23).

Next the father turns his attention to speech or the

mouth. He urges his child to avoid "crooked speech" and "devious talk" (verse 24). Wicked persons are particularly skillful in using smooth words. The fateful powers of the lips must be carefully in tune with a proper heart. Words have the capacity to destroy as well as to create.

Although of lesser importance than the heart or the mouth, the eyes and the feet must be properly directed along the paths of righteousness. The eyes could focus on the wrong objects: the external beauty of the harlot, the seeming wealth of the wicked, the enviable possessions of a neighbor. Without the guidance of a wise heart, the eyes could easily sway one's desires toward the wrong values. The eyes must remain fixed firmly on the higher goals set by wisdom, looking neither to the left nor to the right.

Similarly, the feet could carry a person along the path of virtue or along the path of wickedness. Like the eyes, wisdom must control the feet lest they lead one astray. Without guidance by a heart nurtured in wisdom, both the eyes and the feet may look at and follow the ways of wickedness.

The three instruction units in Proverbs 4 register similar, yet different, points. Verses 1-9 urge loving affection for wisdom, out of a respect for and commitment to tradition. Verses 10-19 command people to follow the paths of righteousness, with clear and forceful direction to one's life. By contrast, the way of wickedness lies shrouded in darkness, concealing the way to disaster. Verses 20-27 describe the roles of different parts of the body and how each part contributes to a righteous life.

The unspoken assumption underlying each of these instructions is the notion of human freedom and the responsibility people have for choosing the right path. Only in a few places does Proverbs not assume human freedom. Otherwise, how is a person to be held accountable for his or her choices? If people have no real part to play in their life, they cannot be held responsible for their actions. Accountability must lie with someone or something else.

In Proverbs 4, however, the writer assumes that people do have the power of free choice, that they have at least two paths to follow, and therefore they can be held responsible for what they do. In order for their children to be able to assume these responsibilities, parents must teach morality to them. While parents cannot (and should not) make all choices for their children, parents must teach proper goals and appropriate behavior carefully. Both tradition and experience attest that wisdom is the only true path to abundant living.

CLOSING PRAYER

O God, grant us an appreciation for the wisdom of our religious traditions, a willingness to accept the responsibility for the moral education of our children, and the courage to be better examples of persons who walk in the ways of wisdom. Through Jesus Christ our Lord, we pray. Amen.

THE VALUE OF WISDOM

PURPOSE

To help us develop a sincere affection for wisdom as an expression of God's creativity

BIBLE PASSAGE

Proverbs 8:22-36

22 The LORD created me at the
     beginning of his work,
    the first of his acts of long ago.

23 Ages ago I was set up,
    at the first, before the beginning of
    the earth.

24 When there were no depths I was
     brought forth,
    when there were no springs abounding
    with water.

25 Before the mountains had been shaped,
    before the hills, I was brought forth—

26 when he had not yet made earth and fields,
    or the world's first bits of soil.

27 When he established the heavens, I was
     there,

when he drew a circle on the face
of the deep,
28 when he made firm the skies above,
when he established the fountains
of the deep,
29 when he assigned to the sea its limit,
so that the waters might not transgress
his command,
when he marked out the foundations of
the earth,
30 then I was beside him, like a
master worker;
and I was daily his delight,
rejoicing before him always,
31 rejoicing in his inhabited world
and delighting in the human race.

32 And now, my children, listen to me:
happy are those who keep my ways.
33 Hear instruction and be wise,
and do not neglect it.
34 Happy is the one who listens to me:
watching daily at my gates,
waiting beside my doors.
35 For whoever finds me finds life
and obtains favor from the
LORD;
36 but those who miss me injure themselves;
all who hate me love death.

CORE VERSE
Hear instruction and be wise,
and do not neglect it.
(Proverbs 8:33)

OUR NEED

The real value of wisdom is that it helps persons achieve a blessed and prosperous life. Its results are the true measure of wisdom's worth. But why is wisdom so valuable? How does it work?

Obviously, many persons in ancient Israel had tested wisdom for themselves and had discovered its incomparable benefits. Yet wisdom enjoyed more authority in the Old Testament than validity from human experience. Wisdom also basked in the sunlight of God's special blessings. In fact, wisdom was one form God chose as a means of revelation. Wisdom disclosed God's moral laws for social relationships. She opened new avenues of understanding that extended far beyond human experience. She possessed the authority of God.

Wisdom observed carefully the ways and will of God as he created the world. She could speak with authority because she experienced divine creation firsthand.

The nature of authority remains an important aspect of our culture. Advertisers use authority figures in their commercials because of the special appeal these persons have. Along different lines, certain professions enjoy authoritative status in our society: physicians, educators, business executives, and so on. No less than ancient Israel, we too are conscious of authority. The higher the level of authority, the greater the credibility. The truthfulness of an idea, of an argument, or of an explanation depends largely on its mode of verification. On what authority is it based? Why is it true?

Consider the sources of authority in your life. Which people do you consider to be most knowledgeable, and why do they command your respect? Can the nature and levels of authority change? Does religion add additional authority?

In early Israel's quest for knowledge, human experience first provided considerable authority for certain ethical values such as diligence, truthfulness, faithfulness, and cautious speech. The Book of Proverbs is evi-

The difference between these persons is striking. They are totally different in their style and appeal as well as in their message. Yet the temptation to choose the other person is quite strong. Both pursue their audience aggressively, and both find ready hearers.

Wisdom offers gifts of incomparable value that lead to life, while the adulterer leads to "the chambers of death" (Proverbs 7:27). These two women are different. We must take care to choose the right one.

What gifts and rewards do you think wisdom has given you?

Theology and Morality

Proverbs 8:22-31 represents the highest point in the development of wisdom. Beginning as a set of moral regulations, the idea of wisdom moved upward toward personification as an early companion of God, watching as he created the world.

The writer has shifted in his conception of wisdom. No longer does he consider wisdom as only a guide to successful and happy living. Here, wisdom is the first element of Creation. Personifying wisdom as God's companion elevates her to a new position of authority and distinction.

Because wisdom was present as God fashioned the skies, molded the earth, sank the seas, created humans, and gifted them with the earth, wisdom understands clearly the principles and orders of the world. Because wisdom "delight[s] in the human race" (verse 31), she brings them knowledge and life. Her instructions are right and true because they come from the lips of God.

This proverb makes clear that the sages in ancient Israel considered it of utmost importance to combine theological belief with proper morality. Such a union not only lent additional authority to the many moral laws gained from experience, it also abolished the notion that religious belief was limited to a devotional expression. Because wisdom had divine origins and was God's first created work, her moral teachings introduced a new element of faith and gave a new dimension to moral instruction. Faith and morality become bound together in the fear (awe) of God.

The language in this proverb is similar to the Creation story in Genesis 1:1–2:4a. As Christians living in the twenty-first century, our views on the process of Creation may be quite different than those of a biblical writer who lived more or less twenty-five hundred years ago. Even though we may not agree on how the earth originated, we certainly can embrace the theological affirmation central to the Creation story, the idea that the world and our existence in it have meaning and value only because of God.

Whether the priestly writer of Genesis or the sage of Proverbs had a correct understanding of the mechanics of Creation is not at issue here. Both writers were making profound affirmations of faith, not recording scientific observations. For both writers, God existed prior to Creation and acted voluntarily to establish the universe. But first he created wisdom, a heavenly companion who rejoiced and played before him as he did his work.

How does this understanding of the Creation story increase the value of wisdom for you?

Creation and Wisdom

The ancient Hebrew conception of Creation elevates the status of the world and distinguishes the place of human beings. Neither in Genesis nor in Proverbs does the biblical writer describe the world as a veil of tears, an abyss of torment, or the scene of a battle between rival gods. Humankind was created in God's image and was given meaningful responsibilities. The biblical writers viewed the universe and human beings as objects created lovingly and intentionally by God.

The Book of Proverbs develops this Creation theme one step further by indicating that God also created wisdom to teach human beings his will. Wisdom provided an authoritative channel of communication with God. The imagery in Proverbs 8 personalizes wisdom and makes God's revelation more concrete and understandable. Like wisdom, Creation means life. In this proverb, as God created the world and all that is in it, he brought life in the company of wisdom.

Wisdom is not equal to God here (or anywhere else), however; she is a creature that God created, and she is subject to God's will. God has created her for the purpose of bringing his word of life to his creation.

Returning to the earlier theme of theology and morality, it is clear that Israelite sages added a new dimension to their moral instruction through their personification of wisdom. The practical day-to-day observations, made believable by common experience, took on new meaning and new authority once the sages understood that wisdom was of divine origin. Apart from the laws of the priest or the announcements of the great prophets, God's revelation had a new form: the counsels of the sage.

We may draw two important lessons from this section of Proverbs 8. First, as Christians, we must be open to new forms of divine revelation. Imagine, for a moment, how impoverished our faith would be if God had not chosen to disclose himself in new ways to human beings.

The sages discovered God in the moral instructions and proverbs taught by wisdom. This new aspect of Israelite faith may have shocked some people and may have been met with strong resistance in some theological circles. But ultimately the rabbis who established the canon recognized the profound truths offered by wisdom and so included her writings in the Scriptures. The rabbis knew, as we must learn, that God's wisdom comes in many forms. While God's words of life and grace may not change, the channels through which these words come to God's people may differ from age to age. The church needs to remain open and vigilant to new ways of God's revelation.

Theological reflection is an important, ongoing, and essential task. Occasionally, I have heard someone say, "Don't give us theology. Just preach the Bible!" Fortunately, the majority of thoughtful Christians understand that not only is the Bible the primary reference work for all Christian theology, it is the prime literary example of theological reflection.

As we mentioned, ancient Israel's theologians subjected the concept of wisdom to considerable theological reflection. As a result, wisdom became the first of God's creation and his principal form of revelation. The Bible *is* theology! The authors of the Bible *are* theologians! When pastors and teachers engage in theological study, they are doing what the writers of Scripture did. They are interpreting God's revelation in language and in concepts that are meaningful to their listeners.

Since Christians believe in God's continuing revelation, the theological task of the church is an ongoing task, always open to new words in new vessels. As in the case of wisdom, God's revelations assume new forms. The theological task is to interpret these new communications.

What forms of revelation do you see God using today? How do you interpret them?

Wisdom Brings Life

The final verses of Proverbs 8 return to the popular instruction form found so often in Proverbs. Here, however, wisdom, not a parent, is the teacher. In verse 32, wisdom issues her call to attention. Verses 33-34 are moral instructions to heed her advice and to watch attentively at her gates. Verses 35-36 provide the motivation for paying attention to her. Heeding her call results in divine favor and life. To ignore her counsel condemns a person to injury and death.

It is a proper and fitting tribute to Israel's esteem for women that ancient Israel's theologians personified wisdom as a feminine companion of God, the first of his creative acts and the delight of his eyes. Her authority stems not only from the practical and successful lessons drawn from human experience she offers, these lessons have sanctions in God's created moral order.

This feminine figure is to be the object of human respect and affection. Wisdom finds pleasure and enjoyment in God's creation and willingly comes to humankind with God's word of life. As God's properly created and duly appointed messenger, wisdom deserved Israel's respect and affection.

How does the contemporary church show its respect for women as messengers of God?

CLOSING PRAYER

Eternal God, open our eyes and our hearts to your new revelations. Help us avoid enslavement to the past, and make us receptive to your words and to your ways. Through Jesus Christ our Lord, we pray. Amen.

Chapter Four

LESSONS FROM LIFE

PURPOSE

To recognize that the biblical writer is giving moral instruction so that we may lead a life conforming to God's will

BIBLE PASSAGE

Proverbs 22:1-16

1 **A good name is to be chosen rather**
    than great riches,
      and favor is better than silver or gold.

2 **The rich and the poor have this**
    in common:
      the LORD is the maker of
      them all.

3 **The clever see danger and hide;**
      but the simple go on, and suffer for it.

4 **The reward for humility and fear**
    of the LORD
      is riches and honor and life.

5 **Thorns and snares are in the way**
    of the perverse;
      the cautious will keep far from them.

6 **Train children in the right way,**
      and when old, they will not stray.

7 The rich rule over the poor,
    and the borrower is the slave of the
      lender.
8 Whoever sows injustice will reap
      calamity,
    and the rod of anger will fail.
9 Those who are generous are blessed,
    for they share their bread with the poor.
10 Drive out a scoffer, and strife goes out;
    quarreling and abuse will cease.
11 Those who love a pure heart and are
      gracious in speech
    will have the king as a friend.
12 The eyes of the LORD keep watch
      over knowledge,
    but he overthrows the words of the
      faithless.
13 The lazy person says, "There is a lion
      outside!
    I shall be killed in the streets!"
14 The mouth of a loose woman is a deep pit;
    he with whom the LORD is
      angry falls into it.
15 Folly is bound up in the heart of a boy,
    but the rod of discipline drives it far away.
16 Oppressing the poor in order to enrich
      oneself,
    and giving to the rich, will lead only to
      loss.

CORE VERSE

*A good name is to be chosen rather
than great riches,
and favor is better than silver or gold.*

(Proverbs 22:1)

OUR NEED

Aristotle, a famous Greek philosopher, once remarked that moral virtues were to be acquired by habit. Basic values such as patriotism, generosity, and friendship were to be taught to youth, then continually reinforced by society. A person learned to be virtuous, he argued, by being virtuous. At least with respect to how children learn certain values, Aristotle made a good point. They must be taught values, and these values must be practiced over and over again.

Many parents know full well, as did Aristotle, that they must teach and reinforce moral values. These parents no longer assume that children, if left to themselves, will grow into ethically responsible and morally sensitive adults somehow. Good parenting means teaching children moral values.

Little agreement prevails about which moral values parents ought to teach, however. Even members of the Christian community disagree over such fundamental moral issues as abortion, capital punishment, and aid for the indigent. These disagreements are pronounced when different religious communities gather to discuss ethical values. Almost all groups agree that we need more moral education in our society, but whose moral values are we to teach?

As members of the Christian community, our first responsibility is to express our love for God through loving God's people. One way we can show our love is by strengthening our efforts at moral education.

We have few better resources for doing so than the Book of Proverbs. It contains an anthology of moral lessons drawn from life, from divine revelation, and from all aspects of human experience. The values the sages proposed have been tested by generations of persons young and old, Christian and non-Christian, male and female. Not only do these values lead to happiness and well-being, they have the full blessing of God. They are clear and easy to learn, and they have a certain literary appeal.

FAITHFUL LIVING

Proverbs 22:1-16 is an example of the wide variety of ethical values that appear in Proverbs and that are drawn from human experience:

- the value of a good reputation (verse 1)
- the equality of rich and poor (verse 2)
- the wisdom of taking precautions (verse 3)
- the rewards of morality (verse 4)
- the need to avoid harm (verse 5)
- the reason for the moral education of children (verse 6)
- the reality of economics (verse 7)
- the certainty of divine retribution (verse 8)
- the need for sharing wealth (verse 9)
- the way to achieve peace (verse 10)
- the secret to winning friends (verse 11)
- the vigilance of God (verse 12)
- the description of indolence (verse 13)
- the consequences of sexual immorality (verse 14)
- the necessity of disciplining children (verse 15)
- the punishment of the greedy (verse 16)

Which of these values do you need to work on in your life?

Good Character Is Important

Virtue still determines good character. The ancient Greeks identified the four cardinal virtues as wisdom, courage, temperance, and justice. Each of these virtues springs from a properly guided and well-trained soul. A person's inner self determines his or her external behavior. Although substantial differences exist between the ethical theories of Plato and Aristotle and the systems ancient Israel used, both systems assume that virtue is a consequence of good character. Good character is not inherited; it must be learned.

Proverbs 22:1 teaches that the virtues of a good name and good standing in the community (favor) surpass great wealth. Trustworthiness, integrity, duty, and honor indicate that the person has good character. The people of ancient Israel took personal names more seriously than we do today. To them, a person's name described his or her character.

In Proverbs 22:4, "humility" and "fear of the LORD" are values that good character produces. People of faith knew what behaviors were expected. They acknowledged in faith that their identity was related to a spiritual kinship with God. Thus they respected their Creator and sought to do his will.

In Proverbs 22:11, proper motives and prudent speech are virtues that are endearing to a king. In verses 4 and 11, virtues result in favorable consequences and therefore are powerful incentives for good conduct. But in verse 1, a good name is more valuable than great wealth. Thus, good character has both concrete and moral value.

Good character is no less important today than it was when Proverbs was written. A good name is a valuable asset, especially in our American economic marketplace. Large corporations as well as small businesses rely on public trust and respect for their success. Major companies often spend millions of dollars to create a positive public image. The smaller the company, the more important a good name is, since such companies often lack the financial resources of larger companies to offset negative publicity.

In a similar way, individuals need to work seriously at maintaining their good name. Unfortunately, too many times character assessments are determined by a person's profession rather than by his or her character. Certain professions are respected while other occupations are suspect. Thoughtful persons may want to reconsider stereotyping professions; assessing the ethical values of the individual member of those professions is more appropriate.

A second aspect of the ethics of virtue is that good character can be taught. Verse 15 underscores the writer's belief that children need to be taught, corrected, and disciplined to avoid the excesses of folly. The Old Testament never assumes that youth are morally pure. They must learn their values.

Do you think parents spend enough time on the moral education of their children? Should the schools assume this responsibility? Why or why not?

The Value of Caution

Verses 3 and 5 urge caution as a virtue. Recognizing danger and taking steps to avoid it distinguish the wise person from the fool. Since the sage stressed human knowledge and understanding as proper piety, a prudent person who could foresee danger and avoid it would be acting in faith. The foolish person, in contrast, either is too ignorant to recognize danger or chooses to ignore it. The capacity for seeing risk and for guarding against danger is enhanced by personal experience and education.

How do you determine what is dangerous? How do you respond to danger signals?

Economic Reality

Occasionally in Proverbs, a saying appears that seems out of place among the moral and religious teachings. Verse 7 describes an economic reality that is unfortunate but nevertheless true: The wealthy dominate the poor, and the borrower is ruled by the lender. This situation does not conform to God's will.

Nevertheless, within earthly society, economic power is

a stark reality. This verse does not appear to moralize or to condemn the rich or the moneylenders. Instead, it simply renders an observation about their power over the poor.

We can make a similar observation regarding economic conditions in present-day society. Economic power rules most of our social institutions as well as our personal, business, and professional relationships. In an economic society such as ours that actually encourages indebtedness, borrowers, in fact, become servants to lenders.

Mismanagement of personal resources can lead to severe financial repercussions. Financial obligations affect other aspects of an individual's life. Personal pride and self-worth suffer a great loss when indebtedness becomes oppressive. Personal freedom to decide and to act is curtailed because of the severe restrictions lenders place on a person's personal and business operations. As our economic condition deteriorates, small frustrations suddenly grow into mountains of anxiety. However lenient or cooperative lenders may be, the economic realities of indebtedness are oppressive.

In contrast to the observation in verse 7, verse 16 announces disaster to whoever oppresses the poor. Likewise, verse 9 suggests that untold blessings come to people who share their bread with the poor. The special concern for the poor and for the oppressed in verse 16 is more characteristic of the Old Testament than is the thought contained in verse 7. Even in Proverbs, God always sides with the poor and looks with angry eyes of judgment at anyone who oppresses the poor or injures the weak.

I always experience considerable personal frustration when I hear someone remark, "The Lord helps those who help themselves." Actually, nothing could be further from the truth in the Bible. The biblical message is that God helps those who are *unable* to help themselves. God always chooses the weak to humble the strong, the poor to confound the rich, and the lowly to shame the proud.

After reflecting on these verses, do you think the biblical writers are too idealistic or too realistic? Why?

A Humorous Remark on Laziness

One of the most appealing aspects of Proverbs 22 is its diversity of style and presentation. We have examined sayings that teach a moral lesson, record an observation about economic reality, urge caution, and issue a warning against oppressing the poor. In contrast to the somber mood of these sayings, verse 13 offers a humorous remark concerning laziness:

> The lazy person says, "There is a lion outside!
> I shall be killed in the streets!"

Lazy persons will invent any excuse to avoid work. Any activity that requires human effort is a problem. So they imagine all kinds of nonexistent dangers. Their laziness becomes the object of ridicule. Readers of this verse laugh at the foolishness of imagining that lions would roam the streets of a city waiting to attack an unsuspecting person.

Moral education was of paramount importance to the sages in early Israel. God demanded proper moral conduct. Wisdom and prudent behavior were considered appropriate acts of piety and devotion. This uniting of morality with faith distinguished the early Israelite sages. They challenge us today to take seriously the ethical demands of our faith.

CLOSING PRAYER
O God, help us become better teachers of your ways, better stewards of your Word, and better agents of your love. Through Jesus Christ our Lord, we pray. Amen.

PROVERBS
IN PICTURES

PURPOSE

To help us realize that we can draw important moral values and spiritual insight from carefully observing human behavior and from examining the realm of nature

BIBLE PASSAGE

Proverbs 30:18-33

18 **Three things are too wonderful for me;**
        four I do not understand:
19 **the way of an eagle in the sky,**
        the way of a snake on a rock,
    the way of a ship on the high seas,
        and the way of a man with a girl.

20 **This is the way of an adulteress:**
        she eats, and wipes her mouth,
        and says, "I have done no wrong."

21 **Under three things the earth trembles;**
        under four it cannot bear up:
22 **a slave when he becomes king,**
        and a fool when glutted with food;

23 an unloved woman when she gets
        a husband,
    and a maid when she succeeds her
        mistress.

24 Four things on earth are small,
        yet they are exceedingly wise:
25 the ants are a people without strength,
        yet they provide their food in the summer;
26 the badgers are a people without power,
        yet they make their homes in the rocks;
27 the locusts have no king,
        yet all of them march in rank;
28 the lizard can be grasped in the hand,
        yet it is found in kings' palaces.
29 Three things are stately in their stride;
        four are stately in their gait:
30 the lion, which is mightiest among wild
        animals
    and does not turn back before any;
31 the strutting rooster, the he-goat,
        and a king striding before his people.

32 If you have been foolish, exalting yourself,
        or if you have been devising evil,
        put your hand on your mouth.
33 For as pressing milk produces curds,
        and pressing the nose produces blood,
        so pressing anger produces strife.

CORE VERSE

If you have been foolish, exalting yourself,
or if you have been devising evil,
put your hand on your mouth.

(Proverbs 30:32)

OUR NEED

Ancient Israel appreciated nature, since it was the product of God's creative handiwork. In both of the Creation accounts in Genesis, the authors celebrate the majesty of Creation as a deliberate and purposeful act by God.

Even so, early Israel consciously resisted any easy identification of nature with God. Unlike her Canaanite neighbors, Israel drew a sharp distinction between God and the things created by God. She explicitly prohibited worshiping any object of nature (Exodus 20:4) and avoided equating the elements of nature, such as the sun and the moon, with God or even depicting them as an aspect of God's character. God is the Creator of nature, not part of a created nature.

Yet nature is God's purposeful handiwork. Out of chaos and cosmic disorder, God fashioned the world and endowed it with meaning and value. Likewise, God placed humankind on earth and gave them meaningful responsibilities. Laws governed the operations of nature and also pertained to social interaction.

Israel's sages quickly learned that valuable lessons could be drawn from carefully observing both nature and human social relationships. As the products of God's creative efforts, both nature and humankind revealed important aspects of God's will. The sages became careful observers of nature and monitored closely the different forms of human behavior. From these observations they drew important conclusions about nature, about ethics, about politics, and about society.

On a much broader scale, using more sophisticated techniques of observation and analysis, today's natural and social scientists employ similar methods of acquiring knowledge. These scientists observe the natural world and study human behavior. Using this data, they formulate hypotheses about complex natural laws and social structures. These hypotheses are tested again and again, then verified or negated or modified. The scientists then draw conclusions on the basis of their investigations.

Modern scientists do not begin with a theological presupposition about Creation as did ancient Israel's sages. Also, modern understandings of cause and effect are not set within a theological framework. These differences are interesting, but the important point is that both groups used observation as the beginning of knowledge.

Knowledge of God's orders need not always come from the words of prophets or priests, of pastors or teachers. Each of us, through careful observation, can discover important truths on our own. Scientists and sages alike begin with observing behavior. Theologically speaking, this interest in God's creation as a source of knowledge is a source of moral values and spiritual insight.

FAITHFUL LIVING

The wisdom and cleverness of the sages did not end with merely observing the natural and social orders and drawing appropriate conclusions. The sages used creative and highly imaginative literary and oral forms to express their conclusions. Among the most appealing of these literary forms is the numerical style of Proverbs 30. Unlike many other forms used by ancient Israel's sages, the numerical saying does not seem to have had extensive circulation in the ancient Near East. But in the Old Testament, numerical sayings appear in a variety of contexts: Job 33:14-18; Psalm 62:11-12; Proverbs 6:16-19; Amos 1–2.

The numerical style may be related to the riddle in that they both pose questions and then offer answers. Whatever their literary origin, they are useful teaching tools. They are brief, easily memorized, and tasteful. Yet they discuss matters of considerable importance to moral development.

What modern proverbs have you found useful?

Enigmas of Nature

Proverbs 30:18-19 identifies four events of nature that seem to defy human comprehension. They were marvelous to behold and full of fascination, yet they also were difficult to understand. The only response was a sense of wonder and awe.

Observing flight must have enchanted our ancient sage, while perplexing him at the same time. To soar high above the trees, across broad rivers, and over tall mountains with only a slight movement of wings certainly bordered on the miraculous. The eagle in flight is a picture of grace and beauty. It is not difficult to imagine the overwhelming sense of envy the ancient sage must have felt as he stood and watched the miracle of flight.

No less amazing was watching a snake, without legs, slide over a rock without slipping. How did the serpent grip the smooth surface? What means of self-propulsion did it use? After all, other animals have clearly apparent means of locomotion such as legs, fins, and wings. But the snake, with none of these, still is able to move easily on a slippery surface.

A floating ship on the high seas was a third mystery of nature. When the writer threw rocks into the water, they sank. When he plunged into water, he sank too. Yet the ship, larger than either a rock or a person, floated on the waves. How?

Finally, the sage confessed his wonder and amazement at the magic of the sexual attraction that unites a man and a woman. Human love is beyond comprehension, yet it is a source of unending joy and delight. What causes two people to feel such a powerful attraction for each other?

These four mysteries share a common characteristic: While they are clearly beyond human understanding, they are, nevertheless, a source of absolute delight. Perhaps the how and why of these mysteries is not important. In God's wisdom, nature and social relationship occur and often baffle us. But we embrace them in faith and are grateful for them. Sometimes we refer to them as miracles. At other times, we rejoice in our good luck.

Israel's sages bowed in wonder and confessed the limitations of their human understanding. They could only observe and note the mysterious wonder of nature; they could not understand.

Verse 20 is an intrusion into the series of numerical sayings and disrupts the sequence, at least in terms of literary style. However, it describes the baser, less proper aspect of man-maiden relationships. The earlier reference in verse 19 refers to the mysterious but proper sexual attraction between a man and a woman.

Sexual love in proper contexts is beautiful, above reproach, and natural. Adultery, on the other hand, distorts the sexual relationship and perverts the natural impulse into mere animal instincts. Making matters worse, the adulterers arrogantly refuse to acknowledge that what they have done is wrong. Extramarital sexual conduct strains the bonds of social structures and creates tension, anxiety, and mistrust in the parties involved.

The gravity of this moral offense was so great that the sages devoted considerable time writing sayings describing its disastrous effects. The consequences of immoral conduct are grave, and adultery is one of the worst forms of immorality. It is a socially unacceptable distortion of the wonderful way of "a man with a girl."

Which events in nature do we fail to understand even today?

Intolerable Situations

Interrelationships within early Israelite society also provided the sages with subjects for thought. Nature was not the only object of their consideration. The sages frequently pondered the dynamics of human social relationships and noted the circumstances that severed these bonds. Human behavior rarely affected only a single person. Instead, in a group-oriented society such as early Israel's, entire communities were affected by the actions of a single individual.

The sages gradually compiled data on behavior patterns that strengthened social bonds. They also collected information about actions that weakened these bonds. Four such intolerable actions are the subject of the numerical saying in verses 21-23.

Society begins to suffer when political leadership falls into the wrong hands, as when a slave becomes king. As a rule, slaves in the ancient Near East were illiterate, untrained persons who toiled in economic and political bondage. While slaves usually were not mistreated, they were accorded few of the benefits of society. Their major concerns centered on obtaining sufficient food, remaining in favor with their masters, and enduring their hardships with grace.

Clearly, such persons would not be qualified to rule. They lacked the vision of national destiny. They lacked diplomatic and administrative skills. They had no social graces to dignify royal occasions. They had no military support or weaponry.

When the lowly become exalted, they often become impressed with their power and their wealth; and they begin to inflict misery on others to retaliate for what they have suffered. Little wonder the sage shuddered at the thought of a slave becoming king. Trained political leadership was essential in those days, just as it is now.

Since a fool usually is so stupid that he is interested only in satisfying his baser physical needs, he thinks all is well when his stomach is full. His false sense of well-being lulls him into laziness. His goals are shortsighted and narrow. He has little understanding of the complexity of human beings.

Loneliness can do great harm to people. When meaningful relationships occur for those harmed by loneliness, often they are unable to respond appropriately. Lonely people may become overly possessive when they experience a meaningful relationship. They may anticipate losing the relationship, so they withdraw to avoid pain. They may lack communication skills. The emotional scars from years of neglect make any new relationship difficult to sustain.

The final situation the sage finds intolerable is when a maid succeeds her mistress. Often a sense of vindictiveness and retaliation motivates the new mistress. She may lack the charm, the grace, and the character of her former mistress. Thus, she is not a worthy successor.

These four intolerable situations disrupt social relationships and weaken the structure of society. They allow the lower, less noble aspects of human nature to surface; and they may provide the opportunity for people to behave improperly.

What intolerable situations are occurring in your life? What do you plan to do about those situations?

Creatures Small but Wise

Physical strength is not always the key to mastering the earthly environment; intelligence and common sense offset limitations in size. The four creatures mentioned in verses 24-28 are superb examples of small but wise creatures. This paradox serves as an incentive to all persons who face seemingly overwhelming physical disadvantages.

The ant, though tiny in size, has the foresight to gather and store food during the summer. The badger, despite its small size, has the engineering skills to create a home among the rocks. Locusts have well-organized communities, despite having no obvious leadership. Small, weak lizards can be found in royal palaces.

The sage's reason for recording each of these observations is to show how intelligence and hard work compensate for any lack of size. They are models for human conduct.

What gifts do you have that make up for any physical skills you may lack? How can a small membership church succeed in its ministry?

Walking With Pride

We say that certain people display a good presence. We mean that they present themselves well by their conduct, their personality, and their intelligence. These people exhibit what we call *class*. Certainly, the way they walk adds to their presence. The numerical sayings in Proverbs 30:29-31 refer to three animals who have stately walks, similar to a king striding proudly before his people.

Few animals display the awesome majesty of the lion, the mighty king of beasts. His regal walk as he glides easily over the plains and among the trees of the forest reflects his pride and sense of assurance. The strutting rooster and the he-goat are leaders of their groups. They walk with pride and dignity. The king, lord of his subjects, moves with self-confidence and authority. An atmosphere of power surrounds these four leaders. As they walk, their subjects gaze and bow in submission.

Which other physical characteristics can you think of that command respect?

Cause and Effect

The final unit in Chapter 30 (verses 32-33) is an instruction. It offers a situation, then urges a behavior. Bragging and plotting of evil need to stop. Excessive actions cause undesirable consequences: Striking the nose causes it to bleed; becoming uncontrollably angry leads to needless violence.

Unlike the numerical sayings that convey their message

indirectly by observation and paradox, the instruction offers specific advice. Each form has its place in the wisdom literature of ancient Israel, and each form makes a significant contribution to its reader's understanding.

How is your study of wisdom literature helping you?

Conclusion

The responsibility for preserving and transmitting a culture's accumulated knowledge is a significant obligation. Whether recording instructions on moral conduct or presenting lessons learned by observing nature, we should be grateful to Israel's sages for the excellent job they did in passing this knowledge to future generations. Few literary forms in the Old Testament surpass the numerical sayings for their appeal and imaginative insight.

Any of the four subjects in this chapter gives ample testimony to the sages' powers of observation, as well as to their literary skills. Even with modern technology, some elements of nature still bewilder our brightest minds. Disruptions of established social structures still distress many persons. Brains still outweigh brawn in successful and happy living. A good presence still carries a leader into the halls of power.

The ability of the mind to probe the mysteries of nature, however incomprehensible they may be, is a divine gift that must not be wasted. For this reason, exercise of reason in the quest for deeper understanding is an act of piety.

CLOSING PRAYER
Eternal God, teach us to look carefully at your world; to observe nature as your creation; and faithfully to record, experience, and preserve the lessons we learn. Through Jesus Christ our Lord, we pray. Amen.
